A special gift to

_____

From

_____

Date

_____

A Pocket Book of Prayers for Men

© 2004 Christian Art Gifts, RSA
        Christian Art Gifts Inc., IL, USA

Compiled by Lynette Douglas
Designed by Christian Art Gifts

Christian Art Gifts has made every effort to trace the ownership of all quotes and poems in this book. In the event of any question that may arise from the use of any quote or poem, we regret any error made and will be pleased to make the necessary correction in future editions of this book.

Scripture taken from the *Holy Bible*, New International Version®. NIV®. Copyright © 1973, 1978, 1984 by International Bible Society. Used by permission of Zondervan Publishing House. All rights reserved.

Printed in Hong Kong

ISBN-10: 1-86920-145-0
ISBN-13: 978-1-86920-145-6

06 07 08 09 10 11 12 13 14 15 – 15 14 13 12 11 10 9 8 7 6

A Pocket Book of Prayers

for Men

christian
art gifts®

Contents

The Lord's Prayer

Our Father in heaven,
hallowed be your name,
your kingdom come,
your will be done on earth
as it is in heaven.
Give us today our daily bread.
Forgive us our debts,
as we also have
forgiven our debtors.
And lead us not
into temptation,
but deliver us
from the evil one.
∽ Matthew 6:9-13 ∽

Confession
and
Repentance

"If my people,
who are called by my name,
will humble themselves
and pray
and seek my face
and turn from their wicked ways,
then will I hear from heaven
and will forgive their sin."

2 Chronicles 7:14

A Prayer for Forgiveness

Almighty Father, teach me to do everything with the utmost sincerity. Save me from posing even to myself. Make my life unaffected, simple and sincere. Cleanse me from selfishness; let my gaze be outward rather than inward. Teach me to think more of others than of myself. Forbid that my own interests should be paramount. Pardon, I beseech Thee, all that is and has been wrong in my life and character. Had I always sought Thy will I should now have been strong in the Lord, instead of being the weak, slothful, vacillating creature that I am. But it is never too late. Help me to remedy the evil and henceforth to build with honesty and prayer. Amen

Walter James

A Confession

If my soul has turned
perversely to the dark;
If I have left some brother
wounded by the way;
If I have preferred my aims to Thine;
If I have been impatient
and would not wait;
If I have marred
the pattern drawn out for my life;
If I have cost tears to those I love;
If my heart has murmured
against Thy will,
O Lord, forgive me.

∽ F. B. Meyer ∽

Repentance

Lord, You know all about my sins,
and the things
I would rather keep from You.
Your goodness shows them
up for what they are.
I admit my wrongdoing,
my treachery, and defiance.
Oh, how long shall the power of evil
lord it over me?
Or have the joy of seeing me stumble?
Lord, Son of David, help me.
In Your great and constant love,
forgive me,
even as You have forgiven me
from childhood until now.
I rely on Your love, Lord.
My heart shall rejoice
for You have set me free.
I will praise and exalt You forever, for
You have dealt so lovingly with me.

Launcelot Andrewes

Repentance

Forgive me, dear Lord, for the sins that
come to my remembrance when I turn to
confession.
I have been slack in prayer and slow
to witness.
I have shown resentment at criticism.
I have been irritable and impatient even
over trifles.
I have been self-indulgent and allowed
words and feelings to get out of control.
I have quarreled and been slow to make
it up.

Confession and Repentance

I have spread fear through my fearing
and depression through my depression.
I have assessed the faults of others as
worse than my own without due thought
of my privileges and without knowledge
of their hard way.
O Thou, before whom my heart is laid
open and bare, forgive me, and help me
to do better.

    Amen

◦ Leslie Weatherhead ◦

David's Confession

Have mercy on me, O God,
  according to your
    unfailing love;
according to your great
      compassion
    blot out my
      transgressions.
Wash away all my iniquity
    and cleanse me from
      my sin.
For I know my transgressions,
    and my sin is always
      before me.
Against you, you only,
      have I sinned
    and done what is evil
      in your sight,
so that you are proved right
      when you speak
    and justified when
      you judge.

Confession and Repentance

Surely I was sinful at birth,
    sinful from the time my
        mother conceived me.
Surely you desire truth in the
        inner parts;
    you teach me wisdom in
        the inmost place.
Cleanse me with hyssop, and
        I will be clean;
    wash me, and I will be
        whiter than snow.
Let me hear joy and gladness;
    let the bones you have
        crushed rejoice.
Hide your face from my sins
    and blot out all my iniquity.
Create in me a pure heart, O God,
    and renew a steadfast spirit
        within me.

Psalm 51:1-10

Cleanse Our Thoughts

Almighty God,
Unto whom all hearts be open,
all desires known,
and from whom no secrets are hid;
cleanse the thoughts of our hearts
by the inspiration of the Holy Spirit,
that we may perfectly love Thee
and worthily magnify Thy holy name.
Through Christ our Lord.
Amen

The Book of Common Prayer

A Plea for Mercy

O Lord, in whose hands are life and death, by whose power I am sustained, and by whose mercy I am spared, look down upon me with pity. Forgive me that I have until now so much neglected the duty which Thou hast assigned to me, and suffered the days and hours of which I must give account to pass away without any endeavor to accomplish Thy will.

Make me to remember, O God, that every day is Thy gift and ought to be used according to Thy command. Grant me, therefore, so to repent of my negligence that I may obtain mercy from Thee, and pass the time which Thou shalt yet allow me in diligent performance of Thy commands, through Jesus Christ.

⚮ Samuel Johnson ⚮

Spiritual
Growth

Going it Alone

Lord, I need others.
The way of man
is too hard to be trodden alone.
But I avoid the hands outstretched
to help me,
I want to act alone,
I want to fight alone,
I want to succeed alone.
And yet beside me walks a friend,
a spouse, a brother,
a neighbor, a fellow-worker.
You have placed them near me, Lord,
and too often I ignore them.
And yet it is together
that we shall overcome the world.
Lord, grant, that I may see,
that I may accept,
all the Simons on my road.

∽ Michel Quoist ∽

Spiritual Growth

We have not stopped praying for you and asking God to fill you with the knowledge of his will through all spiritual wisdom and understanding.

And we pray this in order that you may live a life worthy of the Lord and may please him in every way: bearing fruit in every good work, growing in the knowledge of God, being strengthened with all power according to his glorious might so that you may have great endurance and patience, and joyfully giving thanks to the Father.

⤳ Colossians 1:9-12 ⤳

Teach Us to Pray

Lord, teach us to pray. Some of us are not
skilled in the art of prayer. As we draw
near to Thee in thought, our spirits long
for Thy Spirit, and reach out for Thee,
longing to feel Thee near.

    We know not how to express the
deepest emotions that lie hidden in our
hearts.

Spiritual Growth

We would not be ignorant in prayer,
and, like children, only make want lists
for Thee. Rather, we pray that Thou wilt
give unto us only what we really need.

We would not make our prayers the
importuning of Thee, an omnipotent
God, to do only what we want Thee
to do. Rather, give us the vision, the
courage, that shall enlarge our horizons
and stretch our faith to the adventure
of seeking Thy loving will for our lives.
We thank Thee that Thou art hearing us
even now. We thank Thee for the grace of
prayer. We thank Thee for Thyself.

Amen

Peter Marshall

The LORD is near to all who
        call on him,
    to all who call on him
        in truth.
He fulfills the desires of those
        who fear him;
    he hears their cry and
        saves them.

∽ Psalm 145:18-19 ∽

Christ, Our Example

O Lord Jesus Christ, who didst hallow the workshop at Nazareth by Thy labor, and didst choose for Thy disciples men of the fields and of the sea and of the counting-house: grant to all who maintain the fabric of the world by their labor, both integrity in their work and charity toward one another, that our common life may do honor to Thy name.

Bless, we beseech Thee, O Lord, all members of the professions, that they may pursue their several callings with learning, devotion, and skill; and grant that all thinkers and writers, musicians and craftsmen, being taught by Thy Holy Spirit, may enrich our common life with things that are true and lovely, and thus glorify Thy name; through Jesus Christ our Lord.

◈ Unknown ◈

For Constant Improvement

We must praise Your goodness
that You have left nothing undone
to draw us to Yourself.
But one thing we ask of You, our God,
not to cease to work
in our improvement.
Let us tend toward You,
no matter by what means,
and be fruitful in good works,
for the sake of Jesus Christ our Lord.

Ludwig van Beethoven

The Way,
the Truth,
and the Life

O Lord Jesus Christ,
who art the way,
the truth and the life,
we pray Thee suffer us
not to stray from Thee,
who art the way,
not to distrust Thee,
who art the truth,
not to rest on any other than Thee,
who art the life.
Teach us what to believe,
what to do,
and wherein to take our rest.

Erasmus

To Know God

Thanks be to Thee,
our Lord Jesus Christ,
for all the benefits
which Thou hast given us;
for all the pains
which Thou hast borne for us.
O most merciful Redeemer,
Friend, and Brother,
may we know Thee more clearly,
love Thee more dearly,
and follow Thee more nearly,
now and forever.

Richard of Chichester

In His Image

Guide us,
teach us,
and strengthen us,
O Lord,
we beseech Thee,
until we become such
as Thou wouldst have us be:
pure, gentle, truthful,
courteous, generous,
dutiful, useful,
and above all valiant
in all our doings;
for Thy honor and glory.
Amen

⤞Charles Kingsley ⤜

Football Night

In this world, Lord, we each have our place.

You, the far-sighted coach, have planned it for us.

You need us here, our brothers need us, and we need everyone.

It isn't the position that I hold that is important, Lord, but the reality and strength of my presence. What difference whether I am forward or back, as long as I am fully what I should be?

Here, Lord, is the day before me …

Did I sit too much on the sidelines, criticizing the play of others, my hands in my pockets?

Did I play my part well? And when You were watching our side, did you see me there?

Did I catch my teammate's pass and that of the player at the end of the field?

Did I cooperate with my team without

seeking the limelight? Did I play the game to obtain the victory, so that each one should have a part in it?

Did I battle to the end in spite of setbacks, blows and bruises?

Was I troubled by the demonstrations of the crowd and of the team, discouraged by their lack of understanding and their criticisms, made proud by their applause?

Did I think of praying my part, remembering that in the eyes of the Lord this human game is the most religious of ceremonies?

I come in now to rest in the pavilion, Lord. Tomorrow, if You kick off, I'll play a new position,

And so each day …

Grant that this game, played with all my brothers, may be the imposing liturgy that You expect of us, so that when Your last whistle interrupts our lives, we shall be chosen for the championship of heaven.

Michel Quoist

David's Prayer

O LORD, you have searched me and you know me. You know when I sit and when I rise; you perceive my thoughts from afar. You discern my going out and my lying down; you are familiar with all my ways. Before a word is on my tongue you know it completely, O LORD.

You hem me in – behind and before; you have laid your hand upon me. Such knowledge is too wonderful for me, too lofty for me to attain.

Spiritual Growth

I praise you because I am fearfully and wonderfully made; your works are wonderful, I know that full well. My frame was not hidden from you when I was made in the secret place. When I was woven together in the depths of the earth, your eyes saw my unformed body.

All the days ordained for me were written in your book before one of them came to be. How precious to me are your thoughts, O God! How vast is the sum of them! Were I to count them, they would outnumber the grains of sand. When I awake, I am still with you.

Search me, O God, and know my heart; test me and know my anxious thoughts. See if there is any offensive way in me, and lead me in the way everlasting.

∽ Psalm 139 ∽

The Master Carpenter

Lord Jesus Christ,
the Master Carpenter of Nazareth,
on a cross of wood and nails
You have wrought man's salvation;
wield well Your tools
in this Your workshop
so that we who come to You roughhewn,
may by You be fashioned
according to Your will;
for the sake of Your tender mercy.
Amen

Unknown

Open the Eyes of Our Heart

I keep asking that the God of our Lord Jesus Christ, the glorious Father, may give you the Spirit of wisdom and revelation, so that you may know him better. I pray also that the eyes of your heart may be enlightened in order that you may know the hope to which he has called you, the riches of his glorious inheritance in the saints, and his incomparably great power for us who believe. That power is like the working of his mighty strength, which he exerted in Christ when he raised him from the dead and seated him at his right hand in the heavenly realms.

⊱ Ephesians 1:17-20 ⊱

Knowing God's Will

The Way of the Lord

Teach me your way, O LORD,
  and I will walk in your truth;
give me an undivided heart,
  that I may fear your name.
I will praise you, O LORD my
  God, with all my heart;
I will glorify your name
  forever.
For great is your love toward me;
  you have delivered me
  from the depths of the grave.

Psalm 86:11-13

Consecration

Use me, my Savior,
for whatever purpose
and in whatever way You may require.
Here is my poor heart,
an empty vessel:
fill it with Your grace.
Here is my sinful and troubled soul;
quicken it and freshen it
with Your love.
Take my heart for Your abode;
my mouth to spread abroad
the glory of Your name;
my love and all my powers
for the advancement
of Your believing people,
and never allow the steadfastness
and confidence of my faith to abate.

⌁ Dwight L. Moody ⌁

An Eternal Perspective

O Eternal God,
though Thou art not such as I can see
with my eyes or touch with my hands,
yet grant me this day
a clear conviction
of Thy reality and power.
Let me not go forth to my work
believing only in the world
of sense and time,
but give me grace to understand
that the world I cannot see or touch
is the most real world of all.
My life today will be lived in time,
but eternal issues
will be concerned in it.
My business will be with things material,
but behind them
let me be aware of things spiritual.

Knowing God's Will

O God, who dwellest in light
unapproachable,
yet also lives within me,
give me grace today to recognize
the stirrings of Thy Spirit
within my soul
and to listen most attentively
to all that Thou hast to say to me.
Let not the noises of the world
ever so confuse me
that I cannot hear Thee speak.

∽ John Baille ∽

Surrender to God's Will

Lord,
I give up all my own plans and purposes,
all my own desires and hopes
and accept Thy will for my life.
I give myself, my life, my all,
utterly to Thee to be Thine forever.
Fill me and seal me with Thy Holy Spirit,
use me as Thou wilt,
work out Thy whole will in my life
at any cost, now and forever.

⌒ Betty Stam ⌒

Fulfill in Us Thy Purpose

O Lord Jesus Christ,
our Maker and Redeemer,
Thy providence hast made us
what we are:
Thou hast a purpose for us;
Do Thou, O Lord, in Thy mercy,
fulfill in us Thy purpose.
Thou alone art wisdom;
Thou knowest
what may benefit sinners
such as we are;
Do Thou, in Thy mercy,
direct our future
according to Thy will,
as seemeth best in the eyes
of Thy Majesty,
O Jesus Christ, our Lord.

Henry VI

On the Seas of Life

O Lord of the Oceans, my little bark
sails on a restless sea: grant that Jesus
may sit at the helm and steer me safely.
Suffer no adverse currents to divert my
heavenward course. Let not my faith be
wrecked amid storms and shoals. Bring
me to harbor with flying pennants, hull
unbreached, cargo unspoiled.

I ask great things, expect great things,
shall receive great things. I venture on
Thee wholly, fully – my wind, sunshine,
anchor, defense.

The voyage is long, the waves high,
the storms pitiless, but my helm is held
steady, Thy Word secures safe passage,
Thy grace wafts me onward, my haven is
guaranteed.

Puritan Prayer

The Will of God

Blessed Master,
with my whole heart
I thank You for the wonderful lesson
that the path
to a life of answers to prayer
is through the will of God.
Lord, teach me
to know this blessed will by living it,
loving it,
and always doing it.
So shall I learn to offer prayers
according to that plan,
and to find, in harmony
with Your blessed will,
my boldness in prayer
and my confidence
in accepting the answer.

⌁ *Andrew Murray* ⌁

Daily Duty

Cheered by the presence of God,
I will do at each moment,
without anxiety,
according to the strength
which He shall give me,
the work that His
providence assigns me.
I will leave the rest
without concern;
it is not my affair.
I ought to consider
the duty to which
I am called each day,
as the work that God
has given me to do,
and to apply myself
to it in a manner
worthy of His glory,
that is to say
with exactness and in peace.

⤳ François Fénelon ⤳

To Do What Pleases God

Grant me, I beseech Thee, O merciful God, prudently to study, rightly to understand, and perfectly to fulfill that which is pleasing to Thee, to the praise and glory of Thy name.

Thou, O Christ, art the King of glory; Thou art the everlasting Son of the Father.

Amen

Thomas Aquinas

Faithful to His Will

O Lord our God,
in whose hands is the issue of all things,
and who requirest
from Thy stewards
not success but faithfulness:
give us such faith in Thee
and in Thy sure purposes
that we measure not our lives
by what we have done
or failed to do,
but by our obedience
to Thy holy will,
through Jesus Christ our Lord.

Unknown

The Will of God

Blessed Spirit of God,
still our restless souls
with Thy tranquil inspiration,
and give us peace;
enable us to discern
the purposes of God
and to wait patiently
upon His will,
that He may comfort
our hearts and establish us
in His strength.
Bring our conflicting wills
to unity in the will of God,
and knit us together
in one fellowship with Thee.

Unknown

Surrender

O great and unsearchable God,
who knowest my heart
and triest all my ways;
with a humble dependence
upon the support
of Thy Holy Spirit,
I yield myself up to Thee,
as Thine own reasonable sacrifice,
I return to Thee Thine own.

⌒Charles Spurgeon ⌒

Abound in Every Good Work

Blessed are Thou, O Lord, who has
nourished me from my youth up, who
givest food to all flesh.

Fill our hearts with joy and gladness
that we, always having all sufficiency
in all things, may abound to every good
work in Christ Jesus our Lord, through
whom to Thee be glory, honor, might,
majesty, and dominion, forever and ever.

Amen

Unknown

Facing
Difficulties

For Peace

Grant unto us, O God,
Thy peace
which passes understanding,
that amidst the storms of life
we may rest in Thee,
knowing that we are
under Thy care
governed by Thy will,
guarded by Thy love;
so that we may face troubles
and temptations with a quiet heart,
through Jesus Christ our Lord.

∽ Unknown ∽

In **Times** of **Testing**

Grant, O God,
that in this time of testing,
our people may know Thy presence
and obey Thy will;
that with integrity and courage
we may accomplish
that which Thou givest us to do,
and endure that which Thou
givest us to bear.
Amen

Unknown

Deliver Us from Evil

O God, we pray Thee, deliver us and all men from the power of evil:

from the fears and faithfulness of our own hearts;

from pride and all forms of self-deception;

from the misuse of power;

from self-concern and indifference to the needs of others;

from the blindness which sees no difference between good and evil;

and from the sloth that allows evil to pass for good.

When we fail, cast us not from Thy presence, but let Thy forgiveness restore us and Thy power make us brave and loyal.

∽ Unknown ∽

In **Adversity**

O Lord,
Grant us virtue and patience,
power and strength,
that we may take all adversity
with good will
and with a gentle mind overcome it.
And if necessity,
and Your honor require us to speak,
grant that we may do so
with meekness and patience,
that the truth and Your glory
may be defended,
and our patience and steadfast
continuance perceived.

⤫ Miles Coverdale ⤫

Surrender

Lord,
we do not know
what this life
has in store for us,
but be it good or bad,
we are willing
to be used by You.
Use us until
that moment comes
when we go
from service good
to service best –
when You begin
to use us in glory!

Corrie ten Boom

A Strong **Tower**

O merciful God, be Thou unto me a
strong tower of defense I humbly entreat
Thee. Give me grace to await Thy leisure
and patiently to bear what Thou doest
unto me; nothing doubting or mistrusting
Thy goodness toward me: For Thou
knowest what is good for me better
than I do. Therefore do in me all things
what Thou wilt; only arm me, I beseech
Thee with Thine armor that I may stand
fast; above all things, taking to me the
shield of faith; praying always that I may
refer myself wholly to Thy will, abiding
Thy pleasure and comforting myself
in those troubles which it shall please
Thee to send me, seeing such troubles
are profitable for me; and I am assuredly
persuaded that all Thou doest cannot but
be well, and unto Thee be all honor and
glory.

⤳ Lady Jane Grey ⤳

Strength

For Great Endeavors

O Lord God,
When Thou givest to Thy servants
to endeavor any great matter,
grant us to know
that it is not the beginning,
but the continuing
of the same unto the end,
until it be thoroughly finished,
which yieldeth the true glory:
through Him
who for the finishing of Thy work
laid down His life,
our Redeemer Jesus Christ.
Amen

— *Francis Drake* —

For Grace

O Lord our heavenly Father,
Almighty and everlasting God,
who hast safely brought us
to the beginning of this day:
Defend us in the same
with Thy mighty power;
and grant that this day
we fall into no sin,
neither run into any kind of danger;
but that all our doings
may be ordered by Thy governance,
to do always what is righteous
in Thy sight;
through Jesus Christ our Lord.
Amen

The Book of Common Prayer

An Infinite Resource

Almighty God, we respond to Thee in many different ways. Whatever our attitude, Father in heaven, rarely do we think of Thee as practical or relevant to our personal or corporate problems. Help us to understand that Thou art a God who cares – who seeks us – who longs for us. Help us see that Thou art the source of all wisdom and power – that Thou art an infinite resource available to meet our needs.

Forgive our indifference and grant us grace to call upon Thee however great or small our problems. Help us to see in the cross the measure of Your love, Your nearness, Your availability. In the name of Him whose mission was that of a sacrificial servant.

Richard Halverson

Be with Us

Lord, be with us this day.
Within us to purify us;
Above us to draw us up;
Beneath us to sustain us;
Before us to lead us;
Behind us to restrain us;
Around us to protect us.

St. Patrick

A Clear Vision

Dear Lord,
give us clear vision
that we may know
where to stand
and what to stand for,
because unless
we stand for something,
we shall fall for anything.

 ∽ *Peter Marshall* ∽

Lift Us Up

Lord, on the way to goodness,
when we stumble, hold us;
when we fall, lift us up;
when we are hard-pressed
by evil, deliver us;
when we turn from what
is good, turn us back;
and bring us at last to Thy glory.

Unknown

To Do What is Right

Grant, O merciful God, that with malice toward none, with charity for all, with firmness in the right as You give us to see the right, we may strive to finish the work we are in; to bind up the nation's wounds ... to do all that which may achieve and cherish a just and lasting peace among ourselves and with all nations through Jesus Christ our Lord.

⤳ Abraham Lincoln ⤳

Strength in the Lord

In me there is darkness, but with You
there is light;

I am lonely, but You do not leave me;

I am feeble in heart, but with You there
is help;

I am restless, but with You there is peace.

In me there is bitterness, but with You
there is patience;

I do not understand Your ways, but
You know the way for me.

Lord Jesus Christ,

You were poor and in distress, a
captive and forsaken as I am.

You know all man's troubles; You
abide with me when all men fail me;

You remember and seek me; it is Your
will that I should know You and
turn to You.

Lord, I hear Your call and follow.

Help me.

⟿ Dietrich Bonhoeffer ⟿

Consecration

To Reflect the Master

O God, help me all through today to do
nothing to worry those who love me,
to do nothing to let down those who
trust me, to do nothing to fail those who
employ me, to do nothing to fail those
who are close to me.

Help me all through this day to do
nothing which would be a cause of
temptation to someone else or which
would make it easier for someone else to
go wrong; not to discourage anyone who
is doing his best; not to dampen anyone's
enthusiasms or to increase anyone's
doubts.

Let me all through this day be a
comfort to the sad, be a friend to the
lonely, be an encouragement to the
dispirited, be a help to those who are up
against it. So grant that others may see
in me something of the reflection of the
Master whose I am and whom I seek to
serve.

Amen

⟨ William Barclay ⟩

Partnership with God

Lord God and Father, I call upon Thee to
enter all the avenues of my life today and
to share every detail of it with me. Even
as Thou hast called me to share with Thee
Thy life, and all the wonders of it. As I am
entering Thy treasures, Thou must now
come into possess all mine. As I am to
share the destiny, glory, and future affairs
of Thy Son, so would I now have Him
share this small destiny of earth which
is mine, the joys of it, and all its small
matters – that we should be One, Thou
and I, even as we are in Christ.

∽*Jim Eliot*∽

Joy in Simple Things

O God,
Who hast made the heavens
and the earth
and all that is good and lovely therein,
and hast shewn us,
through Jesus Christ our Lord,
that the secret of joy
is a heart
freed from selfish desires:
help us to find
delight in simple things,
and ever to rejoice
in the richness of Thy bounty;
through Jesus Christ our Lord.

Unknown

The Gift of Every Day

Make me remember, O God,
that every day is Thy gift
and ought to be used
according to Thy command,
through Jesus Christ our Lord.

‿ Samuel Johnson ‿

The Things That are Right

Almighty God, the Protector of all who trust in You, without whose grace nothing is strong, nothing is holy, increase and multiply on us Your mercy, that through Your holy inspiration we may think the things that are right and by Your power may carry them out, through Jesus Christ our Lord.

⤳ Martin Luther ⤳

For Humility

Lord,
Where we are wrong
make us willing to change;
and where we are right,
make us easy to live with.

Peter Marshall

Simplify Our Lives

Forbid it, Lord, that our roots become too firmly attached to this earth, that we should fall in love with things.

Help us to understand that the pilgrimage of this life is but an introduction, a preface, a training school for what is to come.

Then we will see all of life in its true perspective. Then shall we not fall in love with the things of time, but come to love the things that endure.

Then shall we be saved from the tyranny of possessions which we have no leisure to enjoy, of property whose care becomes a burden. Give us, we pray, the courage to simplify our lives.

Peter Marshall

A Life of Worship

Eternal God, who hast formed all hearts
to love Thee and created all desires to
be unsatisfied save in Thee, quicken
within our souls a continuing longing to
worship Thee.

Consecration

We bring to Thee our consciences, dulled and insensitive. Quicken them by Thy holiness. We bring to Thee our minds, captured by the trivial and partial. Feed them with Thy truth. We lift before Thee our imaginations, stained by impurity. Purge them by Thy beauty. We lift our hearts, wherein selfishness dwells. Open them to Thy love. Into Thy hands we place our wayward wills. Fashion them to Thy purpose.

Send us from our worship into the affairs of life so strengthened within by Thy Spirit that we may be coworkers with Thee, revealed in Jesus Christ our Lord.

∽ *W. W. Anderson* ∽

"If you remain in me
and my words remain in you,
ask whatever you wish,
and it will be given you."

⇐John 15:7 ⇐

God's Love for Us

Father in heaven!
Thou hast loved us first,
help us never to forget
that Thou art love
so that this sure conviction
might triumph in our hearts
over the seduction of the world,
over the inquietude of the soul,
over the anxiety for the future,
over the fright of the past,
over the distress of the moment.
But grant also that this conviction
might discipline our soul
so that our heart might remain faithful
and sincere in the love
which we bear to all those
whom Thou hast commanded us to love
as we love ourselves.

Søren Kierkegaard

An Un**divided** Heart

Teach me Your ways,
O Lord my God,
And I will walk in Your truth;
Give me a totally undivided heart;
Cleanse me, Lord, I pray;
Remove from me all that is
Standing in the way of Your love.

Eugene Greco

Joyfulness of Heart

We thank Thee, O Lord, for all those
good things which are in our world and
in our lives through Thy love. Save us
from being ungrateful. Save us from
magnifying our sorrows and forgetting
our blessings. Give strength of spirit to
rise into joyfulness of heart. By Thy help
may we learn to live as those should who
have trusted the promises of good which
are incarnate in Jesus, and who know that
in the end love must conquer all.

 ∾ *A. Herbert Gray* ∾

Service
and
Ministry

Shine His Light

Stay with me, and then I shall begin to
shine as Thou shinest: so to shine as to be
a light to others. The light, O Jesus, will
be all from Thee. None of it will be mine.
No merit to me. It will be Thou who
shinest through me upon others. O let me
thus praise Thee, in the way which Thou
dost love best, by shining on all those
around me. Give light to them as well
as to me; light them with me, through
me. Teach me to show forth Thy praise,
Thy truth, Thy will. Make me preach
Thee without preaching – not by words,
but by my example and by the catching
force, the sympathetic influence, of what
I do – by my visible resemblances to Thy
saints, and the evident fullness of the love
which my heart bears to Thee.

John Henry Newman

Understanding God

Gracious and holy Father,
give me wisdom to perceive You;
intelligence to fathom You;
patience to wait for You;
eyes to behold You;
a heart to meditate upon You;
and a life to proclaim You,
through the power
of the Spirit of Jesus Christ, our Lord.

Benedict

Serving God

Teach us, Lord,
to serve You as You deserve,
to give and not to count the cost,
to fight and not to heed the wounds,
to toil and not to seek for rest,
to labor and not to ask for any reward
save that of knowing
that we do Your will.

⮬ Ignatius of Loyola ⮬

A Higher Life

O dear Savior,
be not impatient with us –
educate us for a higher life,
and let that life begin here.
May we be always in the school,
always disciples,
and when we are out in the world
may we be trying
to put into practice
what we have learned
at Jesus' feet.
What He tells us in darkness
may we proclaim in the light,
and what He whispers in our ear
in the closets may we sound forth
upon the housetops.

Charles Spurgeon

To Live with the Lord

How simple for me to live with You, O
Lord. How easy for me to believe in You!
When my mind parts on bewilderment or
falters, when the most intelligent people
see no further than this day's end and do
not know what must be done tomorrow,
You grant me the serene certitude that
You exist and that You will take care
that not all the paths of good be closed.
Atop the ridge of earthly fame, I look
back in wonder at the path which I alone
could never have found, a wondrous
path through despair to this point from
which I too could transmit to mankind a
reflection of Your rays. And as much as I
must still reflect You will give me.

Alexander Solzhenitsyn

The Gift of the New Day

We give Thee hearty thanks
for the rest of the past night,
and for the gift of a new day,
with its opportunities
of pleasing Thee.
Grant that we may
so pass the hours
in the perfect freedom of Thy service,
that at eventide
we may again give thanks unto Thee;
through Jesus Christ our Lord.
Amen

Third Century Prayer

A Faithful Soldier

Lord God,
May I adore You with reverence,
put nothing or no one in Your place;
Neither misuse Your name,
nor be ashamed to admit my allegiance
to You.
Make me kind and affectionate,
patient and gentle;
Help me to enjoy my body in purity.
Give me honesty and contentment,
destroying in me all unreal fantasies,
jealous hope and shameful thoughts.
Let me continue Your faithful soldier
and servant to my life's end.

Launcelot Andrewes

A Life of Service

Father,
Bless to our hearts
this word from Your Word.
Help us to make
our lives count for You.
Help us to serve You
with the strength of youth, …
and the strength of age.
And take us at last
into Your presence,
through Jesus Christ our Lord.

Louis Benes

Petition

Morning Prayer

We give thanks unto Thee,
heavenly Father,
through Jesus Christ Thy dear Son,
that Thou hast protected us
through the night
from all danger and harm;
and we beseech Thee
to preserve and keep us,
this day also, from all sin and evil;
that in all our thoughts,
words, and deeds,
we may serve and please Thee.
Into Thy hands
we commend our bodies and souls,
and all that is ours.
Let Thy holy angel have charge
concerning us that the wicked one
have no power over us.
Amen

Martin Luther

Petition

The prayer of a righteous man
is powerful and effective.

James 5:16

In the Morning

O God, our Father, deliver us this day from all that would keep us from serving Thee and from serving our fellowmen as we ought.

Deliver us from all coldness of heart; and grant that neither our hand nor our heart may ever remain shut to the appeal of someone's need.

Deliver us from all weakness of will; from the indecision which cannot make up its mind; from the inability to say No to the tempting voices which come to us from inside and from outside.

Deliver us from all failure in endeavor; from being too easily discouraged; from giving up and giving in too soon; from allowing any task to defeat us, because it is too difficult.

Grant unto us this day the love which is generous in help; the determination which is steadfast in decision; the perseverance which is enduring unto the end; through Jesus Christ our Lord.

        William Barclay

God Give Us Heroes

God give us heroes!
A time like this demands
strong minds, great hearts,
true faith and ready hands;
Those whom the lust
of office does not kill;
Those whom the spoils
of office cannot buy;
Those who possess opinions
and a will;
Those who have honor –
those who will not lie;
Those who can stand
before a demagogue
and damn his treacherous flatteries
without winking.

Petition

Tall folks, sun-crowned,
who live above the fog
in public duty
and in private thinking;
For while the rabble,
with their thumb-worn creeds,
their large professions
and their little deeds,
mingle in selfish strife, lo!
freedom weeps,
wrong rules the land
and waiting Justice sleeps.

⊱Josiah Holland ⊱

Help for Daily Living

Dear God, You constantly pour out Your blessings on us: help us to be a blessing to others.

You gave us our hands: help us to use them to work for You.

You gave us our feet: help us to use them to walk in Your ways.

You gave us our voices: help us to use them to speak gentleness and truth.

You gave us our minds: help us to think only pleasant, kind thoughts.

You have made our lives pleasant every day with love: help us to make others' lives happier every day with our love.

Help us to please You, Lord. Help us to learn; some little deed to thank You with, instead of words; some little prayer to do instead of say; some little thing to give You because You never tire of giving us so much. Amen

Unknown

A Prayer at Night

Watch Thou, dear Lord,
with those who wake
or watch or weep tonight,
and give Thine angels
charge over those who sleep.
Tend Thy sick ones,
O Lord Christ,
rest Thy weary ones,
bless Thy dying ones,
shield Thy joyous ones.
And all for Thy love's sake.

⤳ Augustine ⤳

In the Morning

Give ear to my words, O LORD,
consider my sighing.
Listen to my cry for help,
my King and my God,
for to you I pray.
In the morning, O LORD,
you hear my voice;
In the morning I lay my
requests before you
and wait in expectation.

Psalm 5:1-3

For Our Nation

O God, whose truth is the only sure
foundation of the kingdoms of men:
pour out Thy Spirit, we beseech Thee,
upon this nation, that it may be a source
of wisdom and strength, of order and
integrity, throughout the world.

Lord, bless this country that there may
be peace and prosperity in all its borders.
In peace, so preserve it that it corrupt
not; in trouble, so defend it that it suffer
not. So order it, whether in plenty or in
want that we may seek Thee, the only
sure foundation of both men and states.
Through Jesus Christ our Lord.

Amen

Unknown

A Vision for Peace

Give us, O God,
the vision that can see Thy love
in the world
in spite of human failure.
Give us the faith
to trust Thy goodness
in spite of our ignorance and weakness.
Give us the knowledge
that we continue to pray
with understanding hearts,
and to do
what each one of us can do
to set forward the coming day of peace.

Frank Borman

Daily Gifts

These are the gifts I ask of Thee,
Spirit serene:
Strength for the daily task,
courage to face the road,
good cheer to help me bear
the traveler's load, and,
for the hours that come
between, an inner joy
in all things heard and seen.
These are the sins I fain
would have Thee take away:
Malice and cold disdain,
hot anger, sullen hate,
scorn of the lowly,
envy of the great,
and discontentment
that casts a shadow gray
on all the brightness
of the common day.

Henry van Dyke

For Good Communication

O Lord, grant that each one who has to do with me today may be the happier for it. Let it be given me each hour what I shall say, and grant me the wisdom of a loving heart that I may say the right thing rightly.

Help me to enter into the mind of everyone who talks with me, and keep me alive to the feelings of each one present. Give me a quick eye for little kindnesses, that I may be ready in doing them and gracious in receiving them. Give me quick perception of the feelings and needs of others, and make me eager-hearted in helping them.

∼ *H. M. Soulsby* ∼

Petition

Give me a good digestion, Lord,
and also something to digest;
Give me a healthy body, Lord,
with sense to keep it at its best.
Give me a healthy mind, good Lord,
to keep the good and pure in sight,
which seeing sin is not appalled
but finds a way to set it right.
Give me a mind that is not bored,
that does not whimper, whine, or sigh;
Don't let me worry overmuch
about the fussy thing called I.
Give me a sense of humor Lord,
give me the grace to see a joke,
to get some happiness from life
and pass it on to other folk.

≈ Traditional ≈

Praise
and
Thanksgiving

Praise the Lord

Praise the LORD, O my soul;
    all my inmost being, praise
        his holy name.
Praise the LORD, O my soul,
    and forget not all his
        benefits –
who forgives all your sins
    and heals all your diseases,
who redeems your life from
        the pit
    and crowns you with love
        and compassion,
who satisfies your desires with
        good things
    so that your youth is renewed
        like the eagle's.

Psalm 103:1-5

A Song of Praise

My heart rejoices in the LORD;
in the LORD my horn is lifted high.
My mouth boasts over my enemies,
for I delight in your deliverance.
There is no one holy like the LORD;
there is no one besides you;
there is no Rock like our God.
He raises the poor from the dust
and lifts the needy from the ash heap;
he seats them with princes and has
them inherit a throne of honor. For the
foundations of the earth are the LORD's;
upon them he has set the world.
He will guard the feet of his saints.

1 Samuel 2:1-2, 8-9

The Glory of the Lord

How many are your works, O LORD!
In wisdom you made them all;
the earth is full of your creatures.
These all look to you
to give them their food
at the proper time.
When you give it to them,
they gather it up;
when you open your hand,
they are satisfied with good things.
May the glory of the LORD
endure forever;
may the LORD rejoice in his works –
I will sing to the LORD all my life;
I will sing praise
to my God as long as I live.

Psalm 104:24, 27-28, 31, 33

Praise the Lord, O my soul;
   all my inmost being, praise
      his holy name.

Psalm 103:1

Sovereign Lord

O Absolute Sovereign of the world!
Thou art Supreme Omnipotence,
Sovereign Goodness,
Wisdom itself!
Thou art without beginning
and without end.
Thy works are limitless,
Thy perfections infinite,
and Thy intelligence is supreme!
Thou art a fathomless abyss of marvels.
O Beauty, containing all other beauty!
Thou art strength itself.
Would that I possessed
at this moment all the combined
eloquence and wisdom of men!
Then, in as far as it is possible here below,
where knowledge is so limited,
I could strive to make known
one of Thy innumerable perfections.

Teresa of Avila

Thank You

Thank You for the tranquil night.
Thank You for the stars.
Thank You for the silence.

Thank You for the time You have given me.
Thank You for life.
Thank You for grace.

Thank You for being there, Lord.
Thank You for listening to me, for taking me seriously, for gathering my gifts into Your hands to offer them to Your Father.
Thank You, Lord.
Thank You.

Michel Quoist

To Give Him Glory

To God the Father, who loved us, and
made us accepted in the Beloved:
To God the Son, who loved us, and
washed us from our sins by His own
blood.

To God the Holy Spirit, who sheds the
love of God abroad in our hearts:
    To the One true God
    be all love and all glory
    for time and for eternity.

Grant unto us, O Lord, this day
    to walk with Thee as Father,
    to trust in Thee as Savior,
    to worship Thee as Lord,
that all our works may praise Thee and
our lives may give Thee glory.

Unknown

To the Glory of God's Name

O most merciful and most gracious God, as Thou hast spread Thy hand upon me for a covering, so also enlarge my heart with thankfulness; and let Thy gracious favors and lovingkindness endure forever and ever upon Thy servant.

Grant that what Thou hast shown in mercy may spring up in duty; and let Thy grace so strengthen my purposes that I may sin no more, but walk in the paths of Thy commandments; that I, living here to the glory of Thy name, may at last enter into the glory of my Lord, to spend a whole eternity in giving praise to Thy glorious name.

Jeremy Taylor

Be joyful always;
pray continually;
give thanks in all circumstances,
for this is God's will
for you in Christ Jesus.

1 Thessalonians 5:16-18

A Prayer of Praise

I turn my thoughts
quietly, O God,
away from self to Thee.
I adore Thee.
I praise Thee.
I thank Thee.
I here turn from this feverish life
to think of Thy holiness –
Thy love – Thy serenity – Thy joy –
Thy mighty purposefulness –
Thy wisdom – Thy beauty –
Thy truth – Thy final omnipotence.
Slowly I murmur
these great words about Thee
and let their feeling and significance
sink into the deep places
of my mind.

Leslie Weatherhead

A Prayer at Day's End

O Lord my God, thank You for bringing this day to a close;

Thank You for giving me rest in body and soul.

Your hand has been over me and has guarded and preserved me.

Forgive my lack of faith and any wrong that I have done today, and help me to forgive all who have wronged me.

Let me sleep in peace under Your protection,

And keep me from the temptations of darkness.

Into Your hands I commend my loved ones and all who dwell in this house.

I commend to You my body and soul.

O God, Your holy name be praised.

Amen

Dietrich Bonhoeffer

Praise the Lord

Praise the LORD.
Praise God in his sanctuary;
praise him in his mighty heavens.
Praise him for his acts of power;
praise him for his surpassing greatness.
Praise him with the sounding
of the trumpet,
praise him with the harp and lyre,
praise him with tambourine
and dancing,
praise him with the strings and flute,
praise him with the clash of cymbals,
praise him with resounding cymbals. Let
everything that has breath
praise the LORD. Praise the LORD.

Psalm 150